First World War
and Army of Occupation
War Diary
France, Belgium and Germany

27 DIVISION
81 Infantry Brigade
Royal Scots (Lothian Regiment)
1st Battalion
12 October 1914 - 31 October 1915

WO95/2264/1

The Naval & Military Press Ltd
www.nmarchive.com
Published in association with The National Archives

Published by

The Naval & Military Press Ltd

Unit 10 Ridgewood Industrial Park,

Uckfield, East Sussex,

TN22 5QE England

Tel: +44 (0) 1825 749494

www.naval-military-press.com

www.nmarchive.com

This diary has been reprinted in facsimile from the original. Any imperfections are inevitably reproduced and the quality may fall short of modern type and cartographic standards.

© Crown Copyright
Images reproduced by permission of The National Archives, London, England, 2015.

Contents

Document type	Place/Title	Date From	Date To
Heading	WO95/2264/1		
Heading	27th Division 81st Infy Bde 1st Bn Royal S Cots. Oct 1914-Oct 1915		
Heading	81st Inf. Bde. 27th Div. Battn. Disembarked Havre From England 20.12.14. War Diary 1st Battn. The Royal Scots. 12th October 1914 To 2nd February 1915 Oct 15		
War Diary	Allahabad	12/10/1914	12/10/1914
War Diary	Winchester	12/10/1914	12/10/1914
War Diary	Havre	12/10/1914	12/10/1914
War Diary	Aire-Sur-La-Lys	22/12/1914	22/12/1914
War Diary	Dickebusch	10/01/1915	02/02/1915
Miscellaneous	Appendix I		
Heading	81st Inf. Bde. 27th Div. War Diary 1st Battn. The Royal Scots. February 1915		
War Diary		06/02/1915	28/02/1915
Heading	81st Inf. Bde. 27th Div. War Diary 1st Battn. The Royal Scots. March 1915		
War Diary		05/03/1915	31/03/1915
Heading	81st Inf. Bde. 27th Div. 1st Battn. The Royal Scots. April 1915		
War Diary		01/04/1915	16/04/1915
Heading	81st Inf. Bde. 27th Div. War Diary 1st Battn. The Royal Scots. May 1915		
War Diary		02/05/1915	31/05/1915
Heading	81st Inf. Bde. 27th Div. War Diary 1st Battn. The Royal Scots. June 1915		
War Diary		01/06/1915	30/06/1915
Miscellaneous	Appendix II		
Heading	81st Inf. Bde. 27th Div. War Diary 1st Battn. The Royal Scots. July 1915		
War Diary		03/07/1915	31/07/1915
Heading	81st Inf. Bde. 27th Div. War Diary 1st Battn. The Royal Scots. August 1915		
War Diary		01/08/1915	23/08/1915
Miscellaneous	Field Returns		
Miscellaneous	Field Return	06/08/1915	06/08/1915
Miscellaneous	For Information of The A.G.'s Office At The Base.	06/08/1915	06/08/1915
Miscellaneous	Field Return	13/08/1915	13/08/1915
Miscellaneous	For Information of The A.G.'s Office At The Base.	13/08/1915	13/08/1915
Miscellaneous	Field Return.	20/08/1915	20/08/1915
Miscellaneous	For Information of The A.G.'s Office At The Base.	20/08/1915	20/08/1915
Miscellaneous	Field Return.	27/08/1915	27/08/1915
Miscellaneous	For Information of The A.G.'s Office At The Base.	27/08/1915	27/08/1915
Heading	81st Inf. Bde. 27th Div. War Diary 1st Battn. The Royal Scots. September 1915		
War Diary		01/09/1915	30/09/1915
Miscellaneous	Field Returns.		
Miscellaneous	Field Return.	03/09/1915	03/09/1915

Miscellaneous	Perforated Sheet Giving Detail of Personnel And Horses Wanting To Complete, Shown On Army Form B.213	03/09/1915	03/09/1915
Miscellaneous	Field Return.	10/09/1915	10/09/1915
Miscellaneous	For Information of The A.G.'s Office At The Base.	10/09/1915	10/09/1915
Miscellaneous	Perforated Sheet Giving Detail of Personnel And Horses Wanting To Complete, Shown On Army Form B.213	10/09/1915	10/09/1915
Miscellaneous	Field Return	17/09/1915	17/09/1915
Miscellaneous	For Information of The A.G.'s Office At The Base.	17/09/1915	17/09/1915
Miscellaneous	Perforated Sheet Giving Detail of Personnel And Horses Wanting To Complete, Shown On Army Form B.213	17/09/1915	17/09/1915
Miscellaneous	Perforated Sheet Giving Detail of Personnel And Horses Wanting To Complete, Shown On Army Form B.213	25/09/1915	25/09/1915
Miscellaneous	Field Return.	25/09/1915	25/09/1915
Miscellaneous	For Information of The A.G.'s Office At The Base.	25/09/1915	25/09/1915
Heading	81st Inf. Bde. 27th Div. War Diary 1st Battn. The Royal Scots. October 1915		
War Diary	Morcourt	01/10/1915	31/10/1915
Miscellaneous	Field Returns.		
Miscellaneous	Field Return.	02/10/1915	02/10/1915
Miscellaneous	For Information of The A.G.'s Office At The Base.	02/10/1915	02/10/1915
Miscellaneous	Field Return	09/10/1915	09/10/1915
Miscellaneous	For Information of The A.G.'s Office At The Base.	09/10/1915	09/10/1915
Miscellaneous	Field Return	16/10/1915	16/10/1915
Miscellaneous	For Information of The A.G.'s Office At the Base.	16/10/1915	16/10/1915
Miscellaneous	Field Return	23/10/1915	23/10/1915
Miscellaneous	For Information of The A.G.'s Office At The Base.	23/10/1915	23/10/1915
Miscellaneous	Field Return	30/10/1915	30/10/1915
Miscellaneous	For Information of The A.G.'s Office At The Base.	30/10/1915	30/10/1915

W095/2264/1

27TH DIVISION
81ST INFY BDE.

1ST BN ROYAL SCOTS.
OCT ~~NOV~~ 1914-OCT 1915

27TH DIVISION
81ST INFY BDE.

81st Inf.Bde.
27th Div.

Battn. disembarked Havre from England 20.12.14.

WAR DIARY

1st BATTN. THE ROYAL SCOTS.

12TH OCTOBER, 1914, TO 2ND FEBRUARY, 1915.

Oct '15

Attached:

Appendix I.

Army Form 2118.

WAR DIARY
or
INTELLIGENCE SUMMARY
(Erase heading not required.)

Instructions regarding War Diaries and Intelligence Summaries are contained in F. S. Regs., Part II. and the Staff Manual respectively. Title pages will be prepared in manuscript.

Hour, Date, Place	Summary of Events and Information	Remarks and references to Appendices
ALLAHABAD 12 X 1914	The Battalion left in two trains for BOMBAY, and embarked on the H.T. ARAGON, less 2 officers and 101 men on H.T. NEURALIA. The officers changes were carried on the latter vessel. The Battalion arrived at PLYMOUTH on November 17th, disembarking on the 20th, and railed to WINCHESTER.	M°r
WINCHESTER.	The Battalion were encamped at MORN HILL until the 19th December, when the 81st Brigade (consisting of 1st Br. The Royal Scots, 2nd Gloucestershire Regt., 2nd Cameron Hders, and 1st A.&S. Hdrs) marched to SOUTHAMPTON. The Battalion crossed to FRANCE on the afternoon of December 20th, landing at HAVRE on the afternoon of December 20th. Strength :- Officers 27*, W.O.1, R.&F. 1010 ɸ	Appendix I * Including Medical Officer ɸ Including 6 A.S.C. drivers Lt. BELL to Sick List 21st December
HAVRE.	The Battalion spent the night in the rest camp at ST ADDRESSE, and entrained at 2 p.m. for an unknown	

WAR DIARY

or

INTELLIGENCE SUMMARY

(Erase heading not required.)

Army Form 2118.

Hour, Date, Place	Summary of Events and Information	Remarks and references to Appendices
	destination.	Myert
AIRE-SUR-LA-LYS 22 XII.14	The Battalion detrained about 4 p.m. and marched to French barracks (CHATEAU MOORE) which it shared with the 2nd Gloucester. During their stay at AIRE, the Brigade was employed in digging a line of trenches. The Battalion in Brigade, marched from AIRE on the 6th Jan. and billeted for the night at CAESTRE. March was resumed the next morning in the direction of MILLEKRUISE. Owing to the block of transport on the road, the Battalion was unable to reach its destination and passed the night in lines and farms in the vicinity of the road. On the evening of the 8th Jan. the Battalion moved into billets at MILLEKRUISE.	CAPT. TANNER to Sick list 30th December. CAPTAINS STEWART and PERRY transferred to 2nd Bn with a draft of 113 m. of The Royal Scots who had been sent to Gloucestershire Regt. while at WINCHESTER. Date of Transfer of Officers 2nd Jan.
DICKEBUSCH 10.I.15	Of 6.30 p.m. the Battalion paraded to take over a section of trenches from the 3rd K.R.R. vacating them, in relief by the 2nd R.S.F. on the night of the 12th Jan.	Bn Hd Qrs. in BOIS CARRE Trenches full of mud & water. Most work before them. Casualties :— 9/F. Parrott and 5 men wounded

Army Form 2118.

WAR DIARY
or
INTELLIGENCE SUMMARY
(Erase heading not required.)

Hour, Date, Place	Summary of Events and Information	Remarks and references to Appendices
13.I.15	Battalion moved into rest billets at WESTOUTRE, returning to MILLEKRUISE, and its former billets, on the 15th Jan.	
16.I.15	The Battalion took over the same line of trenches from the 3rd K.R.R., being relieved on the night of the 18th Jan. by the 2nd R. Ir. F. Trenches improved but much labour required for maintenance and further improvement.	Casualties :- Sgt. Lambert (died of wounds) 3 men killed and 6 men wounded. Pte. Bridges died of Pneumonia. 2Lt. R. APPLEBY to Sick List 16th Jan.
18.I.15	Returned to former billets in MILLEKRUISE.	
20.I.15	Proceeded to [struck through] battn take over former line of trenches, leaving them again on the night of the 22nd Jan. During this tour a great deal of useful work was done in the trenches; including drainage; revetting rebuilding parapets, improving blind batteries, making traverse clearing out and cutting new communication trenches. Hundreds of sandbags were used, and thousands were required. All available stakes and planks used up for revetting purposes, still were urgently wanted.	Casualties :- Killed 2 men wounded :- Lt. C.M.V. BIGIE Bn. Hd. Qrs. and 1 company in support at VIERSTRAAT

WAR DIARY
or
INTELLIGENCE SUMMARY
(Erase heading not required.)

Army Form C. 2118.

Hour, Date, Place	Summary of Events and Information	Remarks and references to Appendices
22. I. 15.	Returned to former billets at MILLEKRUISE.	Sgt-Maj. D.C. THOMSON granted combatant commission 2/I/15
23. I. 15.	Marched to WESTOUTRE and were billeted there until the 29th Jan. Men employed repairing roads. Every man, during the period had a bath & that gave him a change of clothing. Marched back to billets in MILLEKRUISE.	
29. I. 15		
30. I. 15.	Took over trenches but for 24 hours only, being relieved night of 31st Jan. and went to ELZENWALLE in close support.	Casualties - Killed 1 man, wounded 4 men (2 since died) 2/Lt D.R. CURRIE, 2/Lt Hon. J.S. STUART joined 31st Jan. Casualties - Killed 1 officer, wounded, 3 men.
2. II. 15	Returned to original line of trenches being relieved on the night of 4th Feb. Prior to turn of relief, the order was cancelled. Subsequently relief was carried out, but the Battalion remained in outpost as a temporary measure for about 3 hours. The Battalion reached billets in DICKEBUSCH at 3 am 5th Feb.	Draft of 3 officers and 135 men + mules arrived DICKEBUSCH on 2nd Feb. Officers:- 2/Lt J.H. DIXON, 2/Lt W.A. COPELAND, 2/Lt A. MAXWELL

A P P E N D I X   I.

WAR DIARY
or
INTELLIGENCE SUMMARY

Appendix I

Army Form C. 2118.

(Erase heading not required.)

Instructions regarding War Diaries and Intelligence Summaries are contained in F. S. Regs., Part II. and the Staff Manual respectively. Title pages will be prepared in manuscript.

Hour, Date, Place	Summary of Events and Information	Remarks and references to Appendices
	1st Bn The Royal Scots	
	Details of those landing in France with the battalion.	
	Lt. Col. D.A. Callender (Commanding).	
	Maj. G.H.F. Wingate. (2d in Command)	
	Capt. F.C. Tanner	
	" N.H.S. Fargus	
	" A.F. Lumsden	
	" E.J.F. Johnston	
	" H.E. Stanley-Murray (Adjutant)	
	" K.S. Robertson	
	" N.S. Stewart.	
	" B.H.H. Perry.	
	Lieut. T. Bell	
	" G.W.B. Clark	
	" J. Burke	
	" H.F.M.W. Wilmer	
	" D.R. Currie	

Army Form C. 2118.

WAR DIARY
or
INTELLIGENCE SUMMARY

Appendix I (Contd)

(Erase heading not required.)

Instructions regarding War Diaries and Intelligence Summaries are contained in F. S. Regs., Part II. and the Staff Manual respectively. Title pages will be prepared in manuscript.

Hour, Date, Place	Summary of Events and Information	Remarks and references to Appendices
	Lieut. G.W.T. CHREE " A.H. RENNIE. " G.M.V. BIDIE 2nd Lieut. N.M. YOUNG. " E.R.H. BOYD " R. MALCOLM. " W. HARRIS " R. APPLEBY. " D. THOMSON " J. HOBBS. Lieut & Qr. Mr. W.G.H. FAIRALL. Lieut O.J. O'HANLON R.A.M.C. (Medical Officer) 1 Warrant Officer 1004 N.C.Os. and Men 6 A.S.C. drivers attached.	None

81st Inf.Bde.
27th Div.

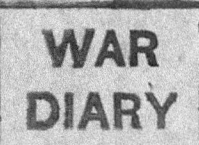

1st BATTN. THE ROYAL SCOTS.

FEBRUARY

1 9 1 5

WAR DIARY or INTELLIGENCE SUMMARY

Army Form C. 2118.

(Erase heading not required.)

Instructions regarding War Diaries and Intelligence Summaries are contained in F.S. Regs., Part II. and the Staff Manual respectively. Title pages will be prepared in manuscript.

Hour, Date, Place	Summary of Events and Information	Remarks and references to Appendices
6.II.15	Battalion took over trenches from 2nd Camerons. 3 Coys. in firing line, 1 Coy. in support with Bn. Hd. Qrs. at VIERSTRAAT	Casualties during this tour Killed 5. Wounded 4.
7.II.15	Bn. Hd. Qrs. transferred to BRASSERIE	
8.II.15	Battalion relieved by 2nd Camerons, and moved back into close support, 3 Coys. at ELZENWALLE with Bn. Hd. Qrs., 1 Coy. remaining at BRASSERIE.	
10.II.15	Battalion moved back to RENINGHELST for 6 days rest. During the rest period all men had a hot bath, and a change of underclothing. The Battalion was employed in cleaning billeting area and in making knife rest entanglements. 2/Lt. MALCOLM and 8 men received instruction in grenade throwing. The G.O.C. 81st Brig. inspected the two drafts on 12.II.15 and expressed himself as being very pleased with the appearance of the men.	Nil

1247 W 3299 200,000 (E) 8/14 J.B.C. & A. Forms/C. 2118/11.

INTELLIGENCE SUMMARY

(Erase heading not required.)

Hour, Date, Place	Summary of Events and Information	Remarks and references to Appendices
14.II.15	Late in the evening the 81st Brig received orders to hold themselves in readiness to move into close support to assist the 82nd Brig if required. The Battalion moved at 10pm towards DICKEBUSCH and was accommodated for the remainder of the night in the hut shelters behind that place.	
15.II.15	Late in the day, the battalion moved into billets in DICKEBUSCH.	
16.II.15	This night the Battalion took over a new line of trenches about ST: ELOI. 3 Coys in firing line and 1 coy in battalion reserve at VOORMEZEELE. Bn. Hd. Qrs. at BUS HOUSE. This section of trenches is in a bad state and difficult of approach. In many cases parapets were not bullet proof, and it made fire could be brought to bear by the enemy. Hundreds of sandbags, and a large quantity of R.E. stores and anything material were carried up to the trenches.	1/1 at

INTELLIGENCE SUMMARY

(Erase heading not required.)

Hour, Date, Place	Summary of Events and Information	Remarks and references to Appendices
	The men worked hard and considerable improvement was made. Much however remained to be done.	Casualties for this period Killed – 5 men
18.II.15	Relieved by 2nd Camerons, and withdrew into close support, 2 Coys. at KRUISSTRAATHOEK CHATEAU and 2 Coys. with Bn. Hd. Qrs. to DICKEBUSCH.	Wounded – CAPT. LUMSDEN and 11 men (1 since died of wounds).
20.II.15	Battalion relieved 2nd Camerons in ST. ELOI trenches. Much work still remained to be done, and work was carried on with vigour. During the relief, LT. H.F.M. WORTHINGTON-WILMER and about 10 men were wounded, and 3 men killed.	Casualties for this period Killed – 8 men Wounded – LT. WORTHINGTON-WILMER & LT. G.W.J. CHREE. 18 men
22.II.15	Relieved by 2nd Camerons. All coys. returned to DICKEBUSCH.	
23.II.15	The men received a hot bath, but no change of clothing.	
24.II.15	Relieved Camerons in same line of trenches. Work of improvement continued. Defence of MOUND specially considered.	

INTELLIGENCE SUMMARY

(Erase heading not required.)

Hour, Date, Place	Summary of Events and Information	Remarks and references to Appendices
26.II.15	R.E. working parties employed at MOUND, and also in digging a new trench which was subsequently found to have been sited too far back.	Casualties during this period Killed :— 11 men Wounded — 16 men (5 since died of wounds) Casualties during this period Killed — [illeg.] wounded — [illeg.]
27.II.15	Relieved by 2nd Camerons and withdrew, Bn. Hq. 2½ Coy. to DICKEBUSCH, ½ Coy. VOORMEZEELE, 1 Coy. KRUISSTRAATHOEK with all machine guns. The 2 platoons from VOORMEZEELE rejoined at DICKEBUSCH at 6 a.m. This night the Battalion withdrew to RENINGHELST for a rest period of 6 days [the Coy. from KRUISSTRAATHOEK and machine gun section moved independently.]	
28.II.15 RENINGHELST	Men employed in improving surroundings of and approaches to their billets. Reliefs of 50 men from 9 a.m to 5 p.m ordered to make knife rests for 1st Ward and following day.	

81st Inf.Bde.
27th Div.

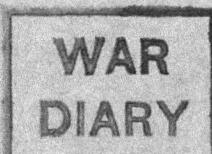

1st BATTN. THE ROYAL SCOTS.

M A R C H

1 9 1 5

INTELLIGENCE SUMMARY

(Erase heading not required.)

Hour, Date, Place	Summary of Events and Information	Remarks and references to Appendices
5.III.15	The Battalion remained at RENINGHELST until 5th March. During this period the Battalion were twice warned to be ready to march at short notice should conditions in the trenches necessitate reinforcement. The Battalion marched from RENINGHELST at 2.20 p.m. halting at the HUT SHELTERS behind DICKEBUSCH for teas. At 5.15 p.m. the leading company marched through DICKEBUSCH to LA BRASSERIE, followed by remaining Coys at intervals of ½ hour, to take over the RIGHT SECTION trenches with Bn. Hd. Qrs. at LA BRASSERIE. Trenches found to be fairly dry in most cases. Improvements carried out. Wooden gratings for trench bottoms placed in position. A pioneers shop established at Bn. Hd. Qrs. and found to be of great use.	3.III.15 2/Lt. D.C. THOMSON to Hospital, sick. Casualties during this period wounded — 4 men. 2/Lt. J.D.C. SCOTT reported for duty 5.III.15
7.III.15	Relieved by 2nd Cameron Hdrs. and returned to DICKEBUSCH	
9.III.15	Relieved 2nd Camerons in RIGHT SECTION Trenches. A quiet night in the whole. Work carried to trenches such as gratings	

INTELLIGENCE SUMMARY

(Erase heading not required.)

Hour, Date, Place	Summary of Events and Information	Remarks and references to Appendices
10.III.15	rifle racks and knife-rest entanglements.	
	Our Artillery shelled the enemy trenches and wire, setting the entanglement considerably, and making havoc with the parapet. Enemy artillery replied, doing little damage.	
11.III.15	Damage to our parapets repaired during previous night. Worn S.A.A. and stores carried up. Actual trenches fairly dry and in best order. Parapets are bullet proof. Artillery bombardment as before. Enemy made a very feeble reply. Relieved by 2nd Cameron Hldrs. and returned to DICKEBUSCH.	Casualties during this period — Killed - 3 men wounded - 10 men
13.III.15	Relieved 2nd Camerons in same section of trenches. No incident of importance. A draft of 87 men arrived during the afternoon, but were left in DICKEBUSCH.	10 men returned from hospital
14.III.15	Orders were received about noon to move tonight further to our right, vacate certain trenches on our left, and take over trenches from the 8th Brig. (Sections L and M) All arrangements made, and guides arranged for.	

WAR DIARY
or
INTELLIGENCE SUMMARY
(Erase heading not required.)

Hour, Date, Place	Summary of Events and Information	Remarks and references to Appendices
	About 5.15 p.m. the enemy opened a terrific artillery bombardment on the trenches in front of ST. ELOI, on the ruined village itself, and thoroughly searched the country between ST. ELOI and VOORMEZEELE. Under cover of this fire, a mine was sprung under the MOUND (S13), followed immediately by an infantry attack which swept over some of the advanced trenches. During the night, a counter-attack was arranged for and our own, consequently, postponed for the night. Battalions in reserve moved up from DICKEBUSCH and work carried out on the G.H.Q. and 2nd lines of defence. The draft was brought out to BRASSERIE. During this afternoon a further draft of 35 men arrived DICKEBUSCH. They were not brought to the trenches During the night affairs were almost normal on our immediate front, and continued so during the following day	15 men rejoined from hospital

INTELLIGENCE SUMMARY

(Erase heading not required.)

Hour, Date, Place	Summary of Events and Information	Remarks and references to Appendices
15.III.15	Relieved in the usual manner by 2nd Camerons, and returned to DICKEBUSCH under orders to be ready to move at shortest notice.	Casualties during period killed – Nil wounded – 6 men
16.III.15	At 2 p.m. the Battalion marched to rest in the ROSENHILL Huts. These huts are built in a small wood, and are both convenient and sanitary. Huts vacated by 9th Argylls.	
17.III.15	Day passed in settling in and making minor improvements. A fine Spring day. County digging up wonderfull.	2/Lt. MAXWELL reopened from hospital
18.III.15 ROSENHILL HUTS.	This night Capts. FARGUS and JOHNSTON proceeded to ST. ELOI to visit the reconstructed section of trenches allotted to the Battalion.	
19.III.15	Battalion proceeded to ST. ELOI section, and took over trenches from 82nd Brigade. Bn. Hd. Qrs. established in the CONVENT, VOORMEZEELE. Division of trenches different from when we last occupied them.	20.III.15. Colonel. H L CROKER to command 81st Infy. Brig. vice Brig. Genl. D. A. MACFARLANE

INTELLIGENCE SUMMARY

(Erase heading not required.)

Hour, Date, Place	Summary of Events and Information	Remarks and references to Appendices
22. III. 15	Left trenches until 23. III. 15; without particular incident.	Casualties during period :- Killed :- 7 men Wounded :- 28 men
23. III. 15	Draft of 90 men under 2/Lt. ROBERTSON and 2/Lt. MUNRO-SMITH arrived. Officers posted to B and D Coys. respectively.	
24. III. 15	Battalion relieved by H.A.C. and returned to ROSENHILL HUTS, (which were shared by 2nd GLOUCESTERSHIRE Regt. B & C Coys billeted in barns) B & C Coys employed in digging on G.H.Q line of defence by night.	2/Lt. J.M. CAMPBELL joined posted to A Coy from 25. III. 15
25. III. 15	A & D Coys. M.G. teams and Signallers similarly employed.	
26. III. 15	B & C Coys. employed in digging.	
27. III. 15	A & D Coys. employed in digging	27. III. 15 Maj. WINGATE and Capt. ROBERTSON visited trenches near YPRES.
28. III. 15	Inspection by G.O.C. V Corps. Divine service. Battalion attached from H.Q. to 82nd Brig. to form reserve for 3rd Division.	28. III. 15 Capt. B.J. COCHRANE, Lt. V.M.G. MENZIES, 2/Lt. M.C. PECKER arrived and were posted to companies as follows :-
29. III. 15	Short route march. Inspection by G.O.C. 81st Brig. Camp divine concert for men of 1st Royal Scots + 2nd GLOUCESTERS	C Coy. Capt. COCHRANE. Lt. MENZIES B. 2/Lt PECKER
30. III. 15	The 81st Brig. detailed for reserve to 3rd Division. Attachment of Battalion to 82nd Brig. ceases.	
31. III. 15	B & C Coys. continued digging operations as before.	

81st Inf.Bde.
27th Div.

1st BATTN. THE ROYAL SCOTS.

A P R I L

1 9 1 5

WAR DIARY
or
INTELLIGENCE SUMMARY

(Erase heading not required.)

Army Form C. 2118.

Hour, Date, Place	Summary of Events and Information	Remarks and references to Appendices
1. IV. 15	The Battalion was inspected by the G.O.C-in-C 2nd Army, in Brigade.	
2. IV. 15	Battalion parade. Companies exercised in making Trenches, parties being told off to revere parapet, close communicating trenches etc. A & D Coys. engaged in digging this night, in same area as before.	
3. IV. 15	Companies exercised under O.C. Coys. in the attack on trenches. 1st and 2nd Bns. played a football match. Result 1st Bn. 1 – 2nd Bn. 0. Battalion marched to POPERINGHE at 5.50 p.m., a distance of about 5 miles, and went into billets there. [Easter Sunday.] Parade service at 11.30 a.m. for C. of S. men.	
4. IV. 15		
5. IV. 15 to	During this period the Battalion remained resting, at POPERINGHE. On 6th April Lt. Col. CALLENDER, the Adjutant, and others and N.C.Os of Companies visited the new section of trenches about to be taken over in the neighbourhood of YPRES.	
8. IV. 15		
8. IV. 15	The Battalion left POPERINGHE [marching by companies] and halted [for teas] at YPRES. Companies left YPRES for the trenches	

WAR DIARY
or
INTELLIGENCE SUMMARY
(Erase heading not required.)

Army Form C. 2118.

Instructions regarding War Diaries and Intelligence Summaries are contained in F. S. Regs., Part II. and the Staff Manual respectively. Title pages will be prepared in manuscript.

Hour, Date, Place	Summary of Events and Information	Remarks and references to Appendices
	independently at intervals of 15 mins. A company at 6.30pm followed by B.C. & D Coys in that order. The new section of trenches is situated some 4 miles due East of YPRES astride the MENIN road. The trenches are in the whole good but much work required to be done in the nature of building traverses and parapets, improving communication trenches and linking up trenches to form a continuous line. The enemy trenches are very close on some portion of our front (within 40 yds), and at another point are fully 250yds distant. Trenches here occupied by A Coy, in the right, C Coy on its left. B Coy in the centre with 1 platoon C Coy i. platoon B W Coy. the MENIN road was C Coys ... Battalion reserve in INVERNESS COPSE. These dispositions held good until the night of 12th April when the battalion withdrew to SANCTUARY WOOD where it remained in close support until 16th April.	Casualties during period — Killed — Capt E J F JOHNSTON (12.IV.15) 4 other ranks Wounded 30 other ranks 11.IV.15 6th Reinforcement draft of 4 other ranks arrived YPRES. Sent to battalion at SANCTUARY WOOD 12.IV.15 14.IV.15 Capt. L.S. FARQUHAR, Lt. G.M.V. RIDIE and 2/Lt W.G. COCHRANE arrived from home. — Capt FARQUHARSON to comm B Coy from 15.IV.15
16.IV.15	Battalion returned to trenches relieving 2nd CAMERON Hdrs, taking over section previously occupied	

Army Form C. 2118.

WAR DIARY
or
INTELLIGENCE SUMMARY
(Erase heading not required.)

Instructions regarding War Diaries and Intelligence Summaries are contained in F. S. Regs., Part II. and the Staff Manual respectively. Title pages will be prepared in manuscript.

Hour, Date, Place	Summary of Events and Information	Remarks and references to Appendices
	The Battalion remained in the trenches until 4.V.15. This tour of duty was not only a long but a particularly trying one to all ranks. The Battalion suffered heavily, losing three officers and 29 other ranks killed and 3 officers and 190 other ranks wounded. The MINNENWERFEN made themselves felt and many men suffered severely from shock. The projectiles from this weapon are very effective in breaking down parapets but are fortunately less so as man-killers. Our trenches were exposed to enfilade fire from a light gun (or guns) and Lt. Young and Lt. Pecker were both killed by shell fire from these guns, as well as several of the men. The enfilade guns could not be located, and consequently, our guns were unable to silence them. The MINNENWERFEN were evidently moved from place to place and thus escaped attention from our batteries.	Casualties:— Killed:— Lt. N.M. YOUNG 23.IV.15 2/Lt. W.A. COPELAND 25.V.15 2/Lt. H.C. PECKER 30.V.15 29 other ranks Wounded:— CAPT. W.S. ROBERTSON 28.IV.15 2/Lt. W.G. COCHRANE 26.IV.15 Lt. G. McBIRIE 3.IV.15 190 other ranks Drafts received 2/Lt. F. CARSTAIRS and 50 men 18.V.15 2/Lt. E.H.M. GEDRGESON (and 17 men rejoined from hospital) 27.V.15

81st Inf. Bde.
27th Div.

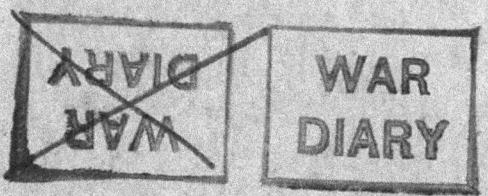

1st BATTN. THE ROYAL SCOTS.

M A Y

1 9 1 5

WAR DIARY
or
INTELLIGENCE SUMMARY
(Erase heading not required.)

Hour, Date, Place	Summary of Events and Information	Remarks and references to Appendices
2. V. 15.	Orders received to vacate our line of trenches and fall back, deliberately, to a new line (only partially constructed) astride the MENIN road and about 200 yds east of HOOGE.	
3. V. 15	Retirement carried out successfully by the following method :— At 10.30 p.m. half the garrison of each trench fell back to ZOUAVE WOOD, through A Coy which held a section of an indifferent line known as the Subsidiary line. At midnight the remaining garrison withdrew from the trenches less 4 men per trench who remained to snipe and fire VERY lights. After the companies commenced their retirement, D Coy from Batt. reserve retired to the new line at HOOGE and occupied the section of trenches immediately astride the road. The trench garrisons having passed through A Coy in the Subsidiary line, this company withdrew, through D Coy, and occupied support trenches in the grounds of the HOOGE CHATEAU. Scouts were left out all night under 2/Lt. CAMPBELL, and fell back upon the new line about 4.30 a.m.	

WAR DIARY
or
INTELLIGENCE SUMMARY
(Erase heading not required.)

Hour, Date, Place	Summary of Events and Information	Remarks and references to Appendices
	reporting that the enemy had then reached CLAPHAM JUNCTION. During the night D Coy worked hard at their trenches with the limited material at their disposal.	
	The night of the 3rd/4th May found the Battalion disposed as follows. D Coy in new fire trenches; A Coy in Support trenches; B and C Coy in Battalion reserve in ZOUAVE WOOD and Hd. Qrs. installed in the old hd-qrs of the 82nd Bing. Telephone communication established to fire and support trenches and to 81st Brigade, but none with reserve companies.	
4.V.15	At 8 p.m. the trenches were relieved by the 2nd CAMERONS and the Battalion withdrew, [by devious and unhealthy routes] to bivouac in the neighbourhood of VLAMMERTINGHE [sounding YPRES by a heavy howitzer needed rest.]	
5.V.15	Battalion enjoyed a much needed rest.	Draft of 90 men arrived and 15 men rejoined from hospital
6.V.15	Bathing arranged for in pond adjoining a farm. As the men had been without a bath for at least 25 days and lacking a change of underclothes for six weeks this was greatly appreciated. By night too men employed as carrying party.	

WAR DIARY
INTELLIGENCE SUMMARY

Hour, Date, Place	Summary of Events and Information	Remarks and references to Appendices
7.V.15	Battalion found party 300 strong (two reliefs of 150 each) to dig and improve a line of defence through YPRES. The party returned without casualties.	
8.V.15	Battalion ordered to form part of Composite Brigade with 2 Coy each 2nd Bn Royal Irish Fusiliers and 2nd Bn Leinster Regt. Lt. Col. CALLENDER to command composite Brigade, with Capt. H.E. STANLEY-MURRAY as Staff Officer. Command of the Battalion devolved upon Major H.F. WINGATE, with Capt. J. BURKE as Acting Adjt. Composite Brigade dispatched at 6 p.m. and the Battalion proceeded with all speed to the ZOUAVE WOOD (HOOGE). Burke Commandant of Lt. Col. CALLENDER.	Wounded.—
9.V.15	By 2 am the battalion was moved up to SANCTUARY WOOD. At dawn the order came to fall back and occupy the G.H.Q. line some 2 miles to the West. This was done. The enemy guns had the range of the lines to a nicety, and put in a number of shells.	Casualties this day. Killed 4 men Wounded. Lt G.M.V. BIDIE 25 other ranks

INTELLIGENCE SUMMARY

(Erase heading not required.)

Hour, Date, Place	Summary of Events and Information	Remarks and references to Appendices
10.V.15	About 6 p.m orders were received to proceed to SANCTUARY WOOD. The battalion arrived down after dusk and were halted at ZOUAVE WOOD. Officers went ahead and inspected trenches held by 2nd GLOUCESTERS, and the battalion took over these trenches before dawn the following day. Disposition of battalion :- A, D Coys fire trenches, B + C Coys support trenches. A message came to the effect that all was not well on the left. B Coy. was ordered to move out to the left in support and to clear up the situation. On arrival it was found that the unit on our left had been driven from one of it's trenches by the combined effect of shells and gas. Seeing the enemy about to occupy the trench in small strength, Capt. FARQUHARSON advanced his company at the double, and the enemy fled in disorder. B Coy had 1 man wounded. The company occupied the trench and proceeded to make the flank more secure.	Killed this day 2 men. Wounded this day - 13 men. (1 since died of wounds)

INTELLIGENCE SUMMARY

(Erase heading not required.)

Hour, Date, Place	Summary of Events and Information	Remarks and references to Appendices
11.V.15	Trenches heavily shelled but with little result. Trenches held A Coy on the right, D in centre, B on left, C in Support. The left company worked hard to consolidate their position which was enfiladed by enemy from the left. Capt. L.S. FARQUHARSON killed in the trench. Shelling continued intermittently all day.	
12.V.15	C Coy relieved B Coy in left trench, B returning to support trench.	
13.V.15	No particular incident to record.	
14.V.15	During last few nights GLOUCESTERS assisted us in digging retrenchment and also diagonal communicating and fire trench continued from front line to retrenchment. The left company suffered very little from enfilade fire or snipers although particularly vulnerable to both.	Draft of 79 men from 3rd Bn. and HQ approved from hospital arrived under Capt. M. HEMBER and 2/Lt. J.F. FINDLAY-HAMILTON (Royal Scots Greys)
15.V.15	A quiet day; some shelling	

INTELLIGENCE SUMMARY

(Erase heading not required.)

Hour, Date, Place	Summary of Events and Information	Remarks and references to Appendices
16.V.15	The draft which arrived yesterday was brought up to the trenches tonight. A further draft of 120 men arrived from 3rd Bn. This draft was intended for the 2nd Bn, but was "diverted" to the 1st Bn. on arrival at ROUEN. No incident to record.	Capt. HENDERSON posted to "B" Coy and 2/Lt. HAMILTON (attached 1st Royal Scots) also "B" Coy.
17.V.15	A day without incident beyond the usual daily shell ration, now greatly reduced.	
18.V.15	This night the Brigade (less 1st and 9th Royal Scots) was relieved by the 3rd Cavalry Division and withdrew to a rest area. The 1st and 9th Royal Scots remained in the trenches under orders of the 82nd Infantry Brigade until the night 22nd May.	20th May. 15 (following officers joined the battalion) 2/Lts J.B. LUMSDEN, J.D. MILNE, R.B. DEVEREUX, K.C. MOTHERSILL
22.V.15	Battalion relieved by WELCH REGT. and moved back to rest area in the neighbourhood of BUSSEBOOM.	Casualties - period 11.V.15 - 22.V. Killed 26 men. Wounded 72 men.

INTELLIGENCE SUMMARY

Army Form C. 2118.

WAR DIARY
INTELLIGENCE SUMMARY
(Erase heading not required.)

Hour, Date, Place	Summary of Events and Information	Remarks and references to Appendices
23.V.15	This afternoon the G.O.C. 2nd Army visited the men informally, and complimented them on the work they had done, and the share they had taken in the operations round YPRES during the past month. Lt. Col. CALLENDER, MAJOR WINGATE and certain other officers having proceeded to England on short leave the command of the Battalion devolved upon CAPT. HENDERSON.	
24.V.15	At 5 am. orders received to hold ourselves in readiness to proceed to YPRES at short notice. The Battalion moved at 4.30 p.m. via RENINGHELST and VLAMERTINGHE and bivouacked about 1½ miles East of the latter place. Here the Battalion remained until the 28th May. This morning the Brigade was ordered to	
28.V.15	move to ARMENTIÈRES. The Battalion marched at 6 am. and reached BAILLEUL shortly before 10 am., going into bivouac just short of that place. The men had a much needed bath.	
29.V.15	At 5 am. the march was continued, and the Battalion bivouacked near STEENWERCK at 9.45 am., passing en route the 11th Royal Scots.	2 Lts. BUCHAN-HEPBURN arrived from England, and 50 men rejoined from hospital. Lt. R.T. MACIVER and E.H.A. TREHERNE from England.

INTELLIGENCE SUMMARY

(Erase heading not required.)

Hour, Date, Place	Summary of Events and Information	Remarks and references to Appendices
30.V.15	This afternoon Lt.Col. CALLENDER, MAJ. WINGATE and other officers returned from leave. Lt.Col. CALLENDER assumed command. Officers from each company proceeded to ARMENTIÈRES to visit trenches of 16th Infantry Brigade prior to taking over. Church parade 11 a.m. At 1-30 p.m the Battalion marched to ARMENTIÈRES and that night took over trenches from the 1/K.S.L.I. and one company of the R.B. Disposition of the Battalion – "C" Coy on the right, "B" Coy, "A" Coy, and "D" Coy. Bn. Hd. Qrs. at FERME DU BIEZ. The first three companies each find their own support, of 1 platoon. The trenches are in the nature of breastworks very solidly constructed, and communication trenches are excellent in every way, affording complete cover from view, even when walking upright.	On first journey, and 2Lt. J.H. DIXSON rejoined from England.
31.V.15	A quiet day without incident, save a few shells in & about Rue del Quz.	

81st Inf.Bde.
27th Div.

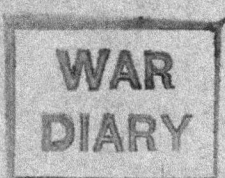

1st BATTN. THE ROYAL SCOTS.

J U N E

1 9 1 5

Attached:

Appendix II.

INTELLIGENCE SUMMARY

(Erase heading not required.)

Instructions regarding War Diaries and Intelligence Summaries are contained in F.S. Regs., Part II. and the Staff Manual respectively. Title pages will be prepared in manuscript.

Hour, Date, Place	Summary of Events and Information	Remarks and references to Appendices
1. VI. 15	The Battalion remained in these trenches without incident and with very light casualties, until the night of the 3rd Inst.	Casualties during period :— wounded 4 men.
3. VI. 15	Relieved by 2nd CAMERONS, and marched to billets in ARMENTIÈRES. Nowhere are the enemy's trenches within 200 yds of our line. Both fronts are well wired and the long grass immediately in front of the trenches was cut (by both parties) to clear field of view. A few rifle grenades were thrown by the enemy but both rifle and gun fire were negligible. Enemy machine guns fairly active spasmodically, but caused no casualties. Relief very easy in account of excellent communication trenches.	CAPT. HENDERSON took over duties of Brigade transp. vice Capt. Holland sick 5th June.
7. VI. 15	Rested in ARMENTIÈRES until 7th June. The Battalion were given baths and change of clothing. Parties supplied for fatigues attending line of defence. Battalion inspected by G.O.C. 2nd Army.	

INTELLIGENCE SUMMARY

(Erase heading not required.)

Hour, Date, Place	Summary of Events and Information	Remarks and references to Appendices
7. VI. 15	Marched to trenches in relief of 2nd CAMERONS. The battalion gave up two trenches on the right and prolonged the line to the left. In one place enemy trenches were within 120 yds of ours, but no extra attention was received from them in this account. Battalion remained in trenches until 13th June. Enemy indulged in occasional shelling of trenches and building immediately in rear, with little result. Snipers fairly active. Grass in front of trenches cut and wire repaired and strengthened. 2 new rifles issued with telescopic sights. Proved to be excellent.	Casualties during period Killed 2 men Died of wounds 1 man Wounded 2 men.
1 Bn. VI. 15	Relieved by 2nd CAMERONS, and marched to billets in C Coy which remained as reserve until night of 16th, being then relieved by A Coy.	Honours and awards — D.C.M. No. 11112 a/Sgt. ANDERSON H. B Coy for gallant conduct near HOOGE. 4/19 X.15

INTELLIGENCE SUMMARY

(Erase heading not required.)

Instructions regarding War Diaries and Intelligence Summaries are contained in F. S. Regs., Part II. and the Staff Manual respectively. Title pages will be prepared in manuscript.

Hour, Date, Place	Summary of Events and Information	Remarks and references to Appendices
	During rest period the battalion availed itself of the baths and carried out a short route march. Digging parties were supplied for work under R.E. in new line.	Honours & Awards. – D.C.M. Under date 12.VI.15, the following appeared, in recognition of work done at ST ELOI (List 33) 9136 C.Q.M.S BRANNAN T. D.C.M 10621 Sgt. HOGG J. D.C.M 7349 a/Cpl. WALLACE T. D.C.M 10362 L/Cpl. WILSON T. D.C.M
20. VI. 15	Relieved 2nd CAMERONS, moving stealthily to the left	Casualties during period
22. VI. 15	Lt Col. CALLENDER assumed temporary command of the 81st Inf. Brig. Battalion remained in trenches until relieved by 2nd CAMERONS 27th June, on which night we retired to billets, less B Coy remaining in reserve. Trenches were shelled on several occasions without much damage. On the 25th Lt R.D. CURRIE and 8 men arrived from ROUEN. Lt CURRIE posted to D Coy.	Killed 1 man Died of wounds 3 men Wounded 2/Lt J HOBBs (since died) 6 men

INTELLIGENCE SUMMARY

(Erase heading not required.)

Hour, Date, Place	Summary of Events and Information	Remarks and references to Appendices
28. VI. 15	CAPT. A.F. LUMSDEN and 1 man arrived from England.	
29. VI. 15	CAPT. LUMSDEN took over command of A Coy.	
	LT. COL. CALLENDER assumed Command of the battalion.	
	During the morning 2 men were wounded by shell fire in ARMENTIERES. The enemy supply the town with a daily ration of "hate" and a few casualties sometimes result, often amongst the civil population. The men have had a bath and change of clothing.	Wounded :– 2 men
30. VI. 15	and have provided two digging parties since the 27th. D Coy. relieved B Coy as reserve to 2nd CAMERONS	Wounded :– 1 man

A P P E N D I X   II.

INTELLIGENCE SUMMARY

(Erase heading not required.)

Summaries are contained in F. S. Regs., Part II. and the Staff Manual respectively. Title pages will be prepared in manuscript.

Hour, Date, Place	Summary of Events and Information	Remarks and references to Appendices
	Appendix "I"	

Mentioned in despatches dated 31st May, for distinguished and gallant conduct in the field. List G d/22/ⅫI/15

Lt. Col. D. A. CALLENDER.
Capt. N. S. FARGUS
Lt. N. M. YOUNG
2.Lt. J. HOBBS
Capt. E. J. F. JOHNSTON.
R.Q.M.S. J. D. WILLIAMS.
6331 Sgt. CAMPBELL C Coy.
9545 L.Cpl. SACHS C "
9771 Pte. CLARK A "
10037 " HASTIE A "
9972

81st Inf.Bde.
27th Div.

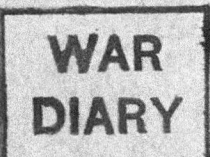

1st BATTN. THE ROYAL SCOTS.

J U L Y

1 9 1 5

Army Form C. 2118.

WAR DIARY
or
INTELLIGENCE SUMMARY
(Erase heading not required.)

15599/9

Hour, Date, Place	Summary of Events and Information	Remarks and references to Appendices
3. VII.15	Took over trenches 65, 66, 67 & 68 from 2nd CAMERONS. Remained in trenches until night of 9th-10th. Enemy Snipers active, our own claimed some success. Trench 67 shelled by enemy, but little damage done. Trench 65 received some attention without much result. Returned to billets in ARMENTIERES, A Coy remaining as reserve to 2nd CAMERONS.	Casualties during period:— Wounded:— 3 men. Drafts received:— 2. VII. 16 men. 7. VII. 41 men. 10. VII. 4 men.
9. VII. 15		
12. VII. 15	"C" Coy relieved "A" Coy as reserve to 2nd CAMERONS. During rest period, the Queen Pipe Band was re-organized. Battalion relieved 2nd CAMERONS in trenches 65, 66, 67, 68.	
15. VII. 15	During the rest period the battalion found working and carrying parties for R.E. and Smoke helmets were sprayed with a solution of a new reagent. The men received a bath and change of clothing. Battalion carried out a route march on the 14th.	

Army Form C. 2118.

WAR DIARY
or
INTELLIGENCE SUMMARY

(Erase heading not required.)

Instructions regarding War Diaries and Intelligence Summaries are contained in F.S. Regs., Part II. and the Staff Manual respectively. Title pages will be prepared in manuscript.

Hour, Date, Place	Summary of Events and Information	Remarks and references to Appendices
19.VII.15	151st Brig. took over trenches 67 & 68. The supporting point at LILLE POST was also taken over by this Brig. The battalion took over trench 67 from the 9th Royal Scots.	Casualties during period:— Wounded:— 5 men.
21.VII.15	Relieved by 2nd CAMERONS, and retired to occupy billets in CHAPELLE D'ARMENTIÈRES. During this time in the trenches, communication trenches were dug from fire trenches to 2nd line, and the wire in front of fire trenches considerably strengthened. Eight dug-outs completed in the 2nd line (PARADISE ALLEY). Remained in billets until the 27th July. During this period working and carrying parties were supplied nightly, smoke helmets sprayed, and men received a bath and change of underclothing. Owing to situation of the billets it was not practicable to carry out a route march.	

WAR DIARY or INTELLIGENCE SUMMARY

Army Form C. 2118.

Hour, Date, Place	Summary of Events and Information	Remarks and references to Appendices
27.VII.15	Relieved 2nd CAMERONS in trenches 64, 65, and 66, B Coy. occupying BOIS GRENIER line. From taking over trenches until the end of the month considerable work was carried out. Wire strengthened and renewed in front of fire trenches and the work of protecting the parapets of fire trenches by throwing earth in front of them was continued on the communication trenches from firing to second line were improved and the main communication trench (COWGATE) prepared in places for lateral defence. The enemy has also been very working and very little rifle fire was employed by either side.	Casualties during period wounded :- 2 men.
31.VII.15	Instructions received to form a Company of Battalion Grenadiers, strength 1 officer, 1 sergeant and 64 other ranks. 2/Lt. DIXON selected for this duty. Artillery demonstration on German trenches at RUE DU BOIS thought about no retaliation.	

81st Inf.Bde.
27th Div.

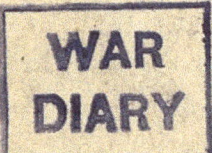

1st BATTN. THE ROYAL SCOTS.

A U G U S T

1 9 1 5

Attached:
   Field Returns.

WAR DIARY
or
INTELLIGENCE SUMMARY
(Erase heading not required.)

Army Form C. 2118.

Hour, Date, Place	Summary of Events and Information	Remarks and references to Appendices
1. VIII. 15.	In trenches T64, T65 and T66.	
2. VIII. 15.	Relieved by 2nd/3rd K.R.R. and marched to billets at FORT ROMPU. Half the battalion were in hut shelters, the remainder bivouacked. The battalion remained at FORT ROMPU until the 16th Aug. By the 12th Aug. enough huts had been completed to house the balance of the men. During this rest period a Grenadier Company of 1 Sgt. 1 Cpl. and 62 Pts. was formed under 2/Lt. Dixson. From 3rd to 7th Aug. the men were exercised at Physical Drill, Drill Control, Coy. drill etc. and a short route march was carried out on the 7th. Work was carried out building butt for a 30yd	Casualties during Rest Period:- NIL.

WAR DIARY
or
INTELLIGENCE SUMMARY

Army Form C. 2118.

(Erase heading not required.)

Hour, Date, Place	Summary of Events and Information	Remarks and references to Appendices
	range by all companies in turn. This was completed on the 11th. From the 9th Aug. to the 14th Aug. an average of 140 men daily were employed in preparing a position at LA VESÉE. On the 10th Aug. "B" Coy were employed in special work at ROLANDERIE FARM. During the week 9th — to 13th Aug. Regimental Games were conducted embracing Boxing, Football, Water-Polo, and Swimming races.	
16. VIII. 15	The Battalion left FORT ROMPU and proceeded to billets at and about ROLANDERIE FARM, remaining in occupation until Aug. 23rd. During this period, working & carrying parties average	

WAR DIARY or INTELLIGENCE SUMMARY

Army Form C. 2118.

Hour, Date, Place	Summary of Events and Information	Remarks and references to Appendices
23. VIII. 15	Strength 1110 men. Men were found daily. Wire parties carried out work in the BOIS GRENIER line by day and night. The Battalion relieved 2nd CAMERON HDRS. in the Left Sector of the new Brigade line, all companies in the fire trenches (T55 T56 T57 and T58) less 1 Platoon D Coy in support at Bn. Hd. Qrs. near BURNT FARM. The trenches were in a neglected condition, and much hard work was entailed to make them strongly serviceable. Actual fire trenches had to be renewed (except T55) and the parados in most cases considerably improved. The wire in front is plentiful and on the whole, in good repair.	

WAR DIARY
or
INTELLIGENCE SUMMARY

Army Form 2118.

(Erase heading not required.)

Hour, Date, Place	Summary of Events and Information	Remarks and references to Appendices
	During the first two days the Battalion suffered somewhat heavily from shell fire, and a small working party working near the main communication trench by night was caught by machine gun fire. Enemy's snipers particularly active, and also their machine guns were unpleasantly busy traversing the top of our parapets by night.	Casualties:- from 23rd to 31st Aug. Killed 2 men Wounded 12 men Carrying parties 16th Aug wounded 1 man 22nd Aug " 1 man Invalided to England sick and wounded during the month of Aug. 25 men Posted from Cadet School 29th Aug. Temp. ?Lt. D. MURCHISON " " R.H. MITCHELL

FIELD RETURNS.

Army Form B. 213.

FIELD RETURN.

(To be furnished by all arms, services, and departments to the A.G.'s Office at the Base in accordance with Field Service Regulations, Part II.)

No. of Report _____ Date. 6th August 1918.

RETURN showing numbers RATIONED by, and Transport on charge of, The Royal Sco... on Gen Service

Detail	Personnel			Animals							Guns, carriages, and limbers and transport vehicles									Remarks
	Officers	Other ranks	Natives	Horses Riding	Horses Draught	Horses Heavy Draught	Pack	Mules Large	Mules Small	Camels	Oxen	Guns, carriages, limbers, showing description	Ammunition wagons and limbers	Machine guns	Aircraft, showing description	Horsed 4 Wheeled	Horsed 2 Wheeled	Motor Cars	Tractors	Mechanical Lorries	Mechanical Trucks	Trailers	Motor Bicycles	Bicycles	
Effective Strength of Unit Details, by Arms attached to unit as in War Establishment:—	25	1001		14	34	20	9					6	5	4		6	2							9	9 Numbers included but not with Lorries
																									Off/1 O.R/3 45
Total	25	1001		14	34	20	9					6	5	4		6	2							9	
War Establishment	29	995		14	34	20	9					6	5	4		6	1							9	
Wanting to complete	4																								
Surplus		6													1									
*Attached (not to include the details shown above)	1	3																							1 bdr Arm. C 1 a.m Sgt 1 Sgt Shoemaker 1 W.O. Cpl 1 Interpreter
Civilians: Employed with the Unit Accompanying the Unit		1																							
Total Rationed ...	26	1005		14	34	20	9																		

* In the case of field ambulances, hospitals or depôts, the number of patients are to be included here, the names being shown in A.F.A. 36.

Signature of Commander. Date of Despatch. 6-8-18

For information of the A.G.'s Office at the Base.

● Officers and men who have become casuals, been transferred or joined since last report.

Place __On Service__ Date __6.8.15__

Regtl. Number	Rank	Name	Corps	Nature of casualty, or name of unit from or to which transferred	Date of being struck off or coming on the ration return	Remarks*
		Wounded, admitted to Hospital :-				
		Other Ranks		2		
		Sick admitted to Hospital -				
		Other Ranks		6		
		Officer granted Sick Leave (indefinitely) by H.O.		1		Lt. Hope
		Sick rejoined from Hospl.				
		Other Ranks		5		
		Transfers to Other Units (Royal Engineers, Gas Co.)		3		
		Draft from Base				
		Other Ranks		4		

*State whether absence is of a permanent or temporary nature, adding, in the case of casuals from wounds or disease, any available information for communication to the relatives.

Copy
True Copy

Army Form B. 213.

No. of Report _____

FIELD RETURN.

_____ CAPT.
1st. IN THE ROYAL SCOTS

(To be furnished by all arms, services, and departments to the A. G.'s Office at the Base in accordance with Field Service Regulations, Part II.)

Date. 13th August 18.

RETURN showing numbers RATIONED by, and Transport on charge of, 1/the Royal Scots at Aix-Noulette

DETAIL.	Personnel			Animals.							Guns, carriages, and limbers and transport vehicles				Horsed		Motor Cars	Tractors	Mechanical			Motor Bicycles	Bicycles	REMARKS
	Officers	Other ranks	Natives	Horses Riding	Horses Draught L.D.	Horses Heavy Draught	Pack	Mules Large	Mules Small	Camels	Oxen	Guns, carriages and limbers, description	Ammunition wagons and limbers	Machine guns	Aircraft, showing description	4 Wheeled	2 Wheeled			Lorries, showing description	Trucks, showing description	Trailers			
Effective Strength of Unit	25	999		55	8		2					6	5	11		6	2							9	9 Members in whole. but not with Bn. Offrs. 1 O.R's 35 X 1 Coy. Run C
Details, by Arms attached to unit as in War Establishment: X 1																									
Total	26	999		55	8		2					6	5	11		6	2							9	
War Establishment	30	995		55	8		2					6	5	11		9	1							9	4 Carts 1 O'Ree Cart
Wanting to complete	4																1								
Surplus		4																							
*Attached (not to include the details shown above)		3																							1 R.A.M.C. 1 Sigs. Intm-ker
Civilians:— Employed with the Unit		1																							1 G. Fr. Cte
Accompanying the Unit																									1 S. Interpreter
TOTAL RATIONED ...	26	1003		55	8		2																		

* In the case of field ambulances, hospitals or depôts, the number of patients are to be included here, the names being shown in A.F.A. 36.

(Sgd) J. R. Callender Lt Col Signature of Commander.

Comdg. The Royal Scots Date of Despatch.

Forms B. 213 / 5

For information of the A.G.'s Office at the Base.

- Officers and men who have become casuals, been transferred or joined since last report.

Place On Service   Date 13-8-15

Regtl. Number	Rank	Name	Corps	Nature of casualty, or name of unit from or to which transferred	Date of being struck off or coming on the ration return	Remarks*
				Sick, admitted to Hospital :-		
		Other Ranks			8	
				Sick rejoined from Hospital :-		
		Other Ranks			6	

*State whether absence is of a permanent or temporary nature, adding, in the case of casuals from wounds or disease, any available information for communication to the relatives.

True Copy.

Army Form B. 213.

FIELD RETURN.

NOT TO BE FILLED IN ~~CAPT.~~

(To be furnished by all arms, services, and departments to the A.G.'s Office at the Base in accordance with Field Service Regulations, Part II.)

Date 20th August 1918.

RETURN showing numbers RATIONED by, and Transport on charge of, 1/5th The York & Lancaster at _____

Detail	Personnel		Animals							Guns, carriages, and limbers and transport vehicles				Horsed		Motor Cars	Tractors	Mechanical		Trailers	Motor Bicycles	Bicycles	Remarks
			Horses			Mules												Lorries, showing description	Trucks, showing description				
	Officers	Other ranks	Natives	Riding	Draught	Heavy Draught	Pack	Large	Small	Camels	Oxen	Guns, carriages and limbers, showing description	Ammunition wagons and limbers	Machine guns	Aircraft, showing description	4 Wheeled	2 Wheeled							
Effective Strength of Unit Details, by Arms attached to unit as in War Establishment:—	25 /1000 *1	26 /1000		55	8	2						6	5	4		6	2							9	9 Number not yet approved of. *1 Lt Col on leave
Total	26 /1000			55	8	2						6	5	4		6	2							9	
War Establishment	30 995			55	8	2						6	5	4		6	1							9	
Wanting to complete	4	-		-	-	-						-	-	-		-	-							-	*1 Officer
Surplus	-	5		-	-	-						-	-	-		-	1							-	
*Attached (not to include the details shown above)	@3																								@1 R.M. Sgt @1 Sgt Shoemaker @1 A/D Cpl @1 B/R Musketry Instr
Civilians:— Employed with the Unit. Accompanying the Unit	@1																								
Total Rationed	26 /1000			55	8	2																			

* In the case of field ambulances, hospitals or depots, the number of patients are to be included here, the names being shown in A.F.A. 36.

(Sgd) E.A. Cathedral M.D.L Signature of Commander.
Monty The York & Lancs

Date of Despatch 20-8-15

For information of the A.G.'s Office at the Base.

Officers and men who have become casuals, been transferred or joined since last report.

Place On Service　　　　Date 20-8-15

Regtl. Number	Rank	Name	Corps	Nature of casualty, or name of unit from or to which transferred	Date of being struck off or coming on the ration return	Remarks
		Wounded:-				
		O. Ranks			1	
		Sick admitted to Hospital				
		Other Ranks			4	
		Sick rejoined from Hospl				
		Other Ranks			6	

*State whether absence is of a permanent or temporary nature, adding, in the case of casuals from wounds or disease, any available information for communication to the relatives.

True Copy

Army Form B. 213.

No. of Report _____

FIELD RETURN.

................................CAPT.
A/Adjt. 1st THE ROYAL SCOTS

(To be furnished by all arms, services, and departments to the A. G.'s Office at the Base in accordance with Field Service Regulations, Part II.)

RETURN showing numbers RATIONED by, and Transport on charge of, 1/9th Royal Scots at _____ Date 27th August 18

Detail	Personnel			Animals							Guns, carriages, and limbers and transport vehicles				Horsed		Mechanical					Remarks
	Officers	Other ranks	Natives	Horses Riding	Horses Draught	Horses Heavy Draught	Pack	Mules Large	Mules Small	Camels	Oxen	Guns, carriages and limbers, showing description	Ammunition wagons and limbers	Machine guns	Aircraft, showing description	2 Wheeled	4 Wheeled	Motor Cars	Tractors	Lorries, showing description	Trucks, showing description	Trailers	Motor Bicycles	Bicycles	
Effective Strength of Unit	25	918			55	8	2					6	5	4		6	2							9	9 Numbers included returned weight Offrs 3 O. Rks 35
Details, by Arms attached to unit as in War Establishment:—	1																								
Total	26	918			55	8	2					6	5	4		6	2							9	
War Establishment	30	935			55	8	2					6	5	4		6	1							9	
Wanting to complete	4	17															1								1 O.R. Sgt 1 Sgt Shoemaker 1 O. Sin Cpl 1 F. Shoemaker
Surplus																									
*Attached (not to include the details shown above)		3																							
Civilians:— Employed with the Unit Accompanying the Unit		1																							
Total Rationed...	26	932			55	8	2																		

* In the case of field ambulances, hospitals or depôts, the number of patients are to be included here, the names being shown in A.F.A. 36.

Sgt J. A. Ballantine 6.6.
Comdg 1/9 Royal Scots

Signature of Commander.
Date of Despatch.

Forms B. 213 / 5

For information of the A.G.'s Office at the Base.

Officers and men who have become casuals, been transferred or joined since last report.

Place **On Service**   Date **27-8-15**

Regtl. Number	Rank	Name	Corps	Nature of casualty, or name of unit from or to which transferred	Date of being struck off or coming on the ration return	Remarks
				Sick admitted to Hosp¹		
				Other Ranks	17	
				Wounded to Hospital		
				Other Ranks	14	
				Sick returned from Hospital		
				Other Ranks	11	
				Killed between date of return on 27-8-15 & 31-8-15		
				Other Ranks	2	

State whether absence is of a permanent or temporary nature, adding, in the case of casuals from wounds or disease, any available information for communication to the relatives.

81st Inf.Bde.
27th Div.

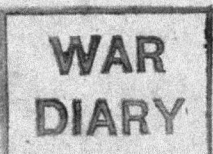

1st BATTN. THE ROYAL SCOTS.

S E P T E M B E R

1 9 1 5

Attached:

Field Returns.

WAR DIARY
or
INTELLIGENCE SUMMARY

(Erase heading not required.)

Army Form C. 2118.

Instructions regarding War Diaries and Intelligence Summaries are contained in F. S. Regs, Part II. and the Staff Manual respectively. Title pages will be prepared in manuscript.

Hour, Date, Place	Summary of Events and Information	Remarks and references to Appendices
1. IX. 15	Batt: still holding line of trenches 55, 56, 57, 58.	Casualties during period 1st – 9th Sept:–
7. IX. 15	Capt. HENDERSON left the Batt. on being appointed Brigade Major of 2nd Brig. The Battalion remained in the trenches until relieved by the 2nd CAMERONS on the 9th Sept.	Killed :– 1 man. Rejoined from hospital.– 7.IX.15 20 men
9. IX. 15	Battalion marched to billets in RUE DELLETRÉE, between the villages of GRIS POT and FLEURBAIX. During our occupation of the trenches, the Companies did much useful and necessary work. The fire trenches with the exception of T55, all required to be revamped. Communication trenches to support line were cut and loopholed to command approaches. New dressing station was built, and weatherproof shelters for S.A.A. and bombs. Officers patrols were particularly active.	

Army Form C. 2118.

WAR DIARY
or
INTELLIGENCE SUMMARY
(Erase heading not required.)

Hour, Date, Place	Summary of Events and Information	Remarks and references to Appendices
	Battalion remained in billets until the 15th Sept.	Casualties from 10th – 14th Sept
	On the 10th and 11th Sept. working parties of about 250 men were found by the Battalion.	Killed – Lieut. R.T. MacIver
	On the 11th Sept. 2nd Lt. MacIver was killed by shell fire whilst conducting a party of Yeomanry round fire trenches to give them instruction in machine gun emplacements etc.	
	The Battalion instructed the 8th and 9th Bn. YORKSHIRE REGT. in various duties connected with trench warfare.	
15. IX. 15	Battalion marched to FORT ROMPU and occupied hut shelters on last occasion.	
17. IX. 15	Marched to billets near VIEUX-BERQUIN.	14. IX. 15
18. IX. 15	G.O.C. 3rd Corps visited the 81st Brig. and they then marched to HAZEBROUCK and entrained for GILLAUCOURT.	Arrival from hospital :– 23 men
19. IX. 15	The 81st Brig. now (with other units of 27th Div.) transferred to 12th Corps, 3rd Army.	

Army Form C. 2118.

WAR DIARY
or
INTELLIGENCE SUMMARY

(Erase heading not required.)

Hour, Date, Place	Summary of Events and Information	Remarks and references to Appendices
20.IX.15	After an uncomfortable journey of 10½ hours the battalion reached its destination at H.30 a.m., and marched a distance of some 6 miles to billets in VARFUSÉE - ABANCOURT.	
22.IX.15	Owing to scarcity of water it was found necessary to move some of the troops from ABANCOURT. At 5 p.m. the Battalion marched to MORCOURT on the R. Somme.	Casualties during period - Arrivals:- 27.IX.15 2/Lt. D.D.A. BERRY arrived, and posted to B Coy.
30.IX.15	Battalion still at MORCOURT. Since arrival, training has been carried out by a series of route marches and tactical exercises.	30.IX.15 Accidentally wounded:- 1 man.

FIELD RETURNS.

Army Form B. 213.

FIELD RETURN.

No. of Report _____ Date _____

(To be furnished by all arms, services, and departments (except A.S.C. units) to the A. G.'s Office at the Base in accordance with Field Service Regulations, Part II.)

RETURN showing numbers RATIONED by, and Transport on charge of, _The Detatchment Service_ at _____ 30th Feb 16_.

DETAIL	Personnel			Animals								Guns, carriages, and limbers and transport vehicles				Mechanical					REMARKS
	Officers	Other ranks	Natives	Horses Riding	Horses Draught	Horses Heavy Draught	Pack	Mules Large	Mules Small	Camels	Oxen	Guns, carriages and limbers, showing description	Ammunition wagons and limbers	Machine guns	Aircraft, showing description	Horsed 4 Wheeled	Horsed 2 Wheeled	Motor Cars	Tractors	Lorries, showing description	Trucks, showing description	Trailers	Motor Bicycles	Bicycles	
Effective Strength of Unit	25	765			55	8	2					6	5	4		6	2							9	1 batt'n came
Details, by Arms attached to unit as in War Establishment:—	1																								
Total	26	765			55	8	2					6	5	4		6	2							9	
War Establishment	30	995			55	5	2					6	5	4		6	2							9	
Wanting to complete (Detail of Personnel and Horses below)	4	30			-	-	-																		at batt'n HQrs
Surplus					-	-	-									1									Office Horse Cart
*Attached (not to include the details shown above)	(1) 3																								Q. O. M. S. I Sgt. Sadd maker 1 O. Ras. Cook 2 L.B. Glenbeau
Civilians:— Employed with the Unit Accompanying the Unit		1																							
TOTAL RATIONED ...	26	769			55	8	2																		

* In the case of field ambulances, hospitals or depôts, the number of patients are to be included here, the names being shown in A. F. A. 36.

For _J. K. Ledbitter_ Lt.

Cmnds. _the 30th Feb 16_

Signature of Commander.

Date of Despatch.

Perforated Sheet giving detail of personnel and horses wanting to complete, shown on Army Form B. 213.

Number of Report _____

Detail of Wanting to Complete			CAVALRY	R.A.	R.E.	INFANTRY	R.A.M.C.	A.O.C.	A.V.C.
Drivers	R.A.								
	R.E.								
	A.S.C.								
	Car								
	Lorry								
	Steam								
Gunners									
Smith Gunners									
Range Takers									
Farriers	Serjeants								
	Corporals								
	Shoeing, or Shoeing and Carriage smiths								
	Cold Shoers								
Wheelers	R.A.								
	H.T.								
	M.T.								
Saddlers or Harness Makers									
Blacksmiths									
Bricklayers and Masons									
Carpenters and Joiners									
Fitters & Turners (R. E.)	Wood								
	Iron								
Fitters	R.A.								
	Wireless								
	Plumbers								
Electricians	Ordinary								
	W. T.								
Signalmen									
Engine Drivers	Loco.								
	Field								
Air Line Men									
Permanent Line Men									
Operators, Telegraph									
Cablemen									
Brigade Section Pioneers									
General-duty Pioneers									
Signallers									
Instrument Repairers									
Motor Cyclists									
Motor Cyclist Artificers									
Telephonists									
Clerks									
Machine Gunners									
Armament Artificers	Fitters								
	Range Finders								
	Armourers								
Storemen									
Privates							50		
W.O.'s and N.C.O's. (by ranks) not included in trade columns									
TOTAL wanting to complete to agree with	Officers						4		
	Other Ranks						450		
Horses	Riding								
	Draught								
	Heavy Draught								
	Pack								

Remarks:—

(a) 1 R. Calledon M.O. Signature of Commander.
from Mr. W. Harford
13th Bn. Unit.
Formation to which attached.
5.9.15 Date of Despatch.

[P.T.O.

Army Form B. 213.

FIELD RETURN.

No. of Report _____

(To be furnished by all arms, services, and departments (except A.S.C. units) to the A. G.'s Office at the Base in accordance with Field Service Regulations, Part II.)

RETURN showing numbers RATIONED by, and Transport on charge of, _the total body at the base_ Date _10-2-15_

DETAIL	Personnel			Animals							Guns, carriages, and limbers and transport vehicles				Horsed		Mechanical					REMARKS
	Officers	Other ranks	Natives	Horses Riding	Horses Draught	Horses Heavy Draught	Pack	Mules Large	Mules Small	Camels	Oxen	Guns, carriages and limbers, showing description	Ammunition wagons and limbers	Machine guns	Aircraft, showing description	4 Wheeled	2 Wheeled	Motor Cars	Tractors	Lorries, showing description	Trucks, showing description	Trailers	Motor Bicycles	Bicycles	
Effective Strength of Unit	2	199			58	8	2					6	5	4		6	2							9	West Lancs
Details, by *Arms* attached to unit as in War Establishment :—		1																							
Total	28	201			58	8	2					6	5	4		6	2							9	
War Establishment	30	195			55	8	2					6	5	4		6	2							9	
Wanting to complete (Detail of Personnel and Horses below)	2	16																							
Surplus																									
*Attached (not to include the details shown above)	x 3																								x 1 O.C. + Maj. + Capt. *Sgt. Instructor
Civilians:— Employed with the Unit Accompanying the Unit	@1																								1 O. R. as Capt. or 2 Lce Cpls
TOTAL RATIONED ...																									

* In the case of field ambulances, hospitals or depots, the number of patients are to be included here, the names being shown in A. F. A. 36.

(Sgd) S. A. Callender Lt. Col. _____ Signature of Commander.

Comdg. The Field Amb. 10-2-15 Date of Despatch.

For information of the A.G.'s Office at the Base.

Officers and men who have become casuals, been transferred or joined since last report.

Place On Service   Date 10th Feby 15

Regtl. Number	Rank	Name	Corps	Nature of casualty, or name of unit from or to which transferred	Date of being struck off or coming on the ration return	Remarks*
				Draft of convalescents from Base		
				Other Ranks	20	
				Sick returned from Hosp		
				Other Ranks	3	
				Sick admitted to Hosp		
				Other Ranks	8	
				Sick of Wounds		
				Other Ranks	1	
				Joined Batln		
				~~Other Ranks~~ Officers	2	2 Lts Murchison Mitchell

* State whether absence is of a permanent or temporary nature, adding, in the case of casuals from wounds or disease, any available information for communication to the relatives.

Perforated Sheet giving detail of personnel and horses wanting to complete, shown on Army Form B. 213.

Number of Report _____

Remarks :—

_____ Signature of Commander.
_____ Unit.
_____ Formation to which attached.
_____ Date of Despatch.

[P.T.O.

Army Form B. 213.

FIELD RETURN.

No. of Report _____

(To be furnished by all arms, services, and departments (except A.S.C. units) to the A. G.'s Office at the Base in accordance with Field Service Regulations, Part II.)

RETURN showing numbers RATIONED by, and Transport on charge of, _the below units_ at _the lines_ Date _17-9-15_

DETAIL	Personnel			Animals.							Guns, carriages, and limbers and transport vehicles						Mechanical				REMARKS
	Officers	Other ranks	Natives	Horses Riding	Draught	Heavy Draught	Pack	Mules Large	Mules Small	Camels	Oxen	Guns, carriages and limbers, showing description	Ammunition wagons and limbers	Machine guns	Aircraft, showing description	Horsed 4 Wheeled	Horsed 2 Wheeled	Motor Cars	Tractors	Lorries, showing description	Trucks, showing description	Trailers	Motor Bicycles	Bicycles	
Effective Strength of Unit	25/000				55	8	2					6	6	5		6	2							9	
Details, by *Arms* attached to unit as in War Establishment :—	1																								1 half A.A.C
Total	25/000				55	8	2					6	6	5		6	2							9	
War Establishment	30/000				55	8	2					6	5	4		6	2							9	
Wanting to complete (Detail of Personnel and Horses below)																									4 horses
Surplus	5											1	1	1			1								Lifford new cast
*Attached (not to include the details shown above)	*5																								* 1 R.A.M.C att 1 Sgt 3 rankers
Civilians :— Employed with the Unit Accompanying the Unit	1																								1/C Rose rifle D.I. for transport
TOTAL RATIONED ...	25/001				55	8	2																		

* In the case of field ambulances, hospitals or depots, the number of patients are to be included here, the names being shown in A. F. A. 36.

Signature of Commander.

Date of Despatch _17-9-15_

For information of the A.G.'s Office at the Base.

Officers and men who have become casuals, been transferred or joined since last report.

Place **On Service**   Date **1st 6 18**

Regtl. Number	Rank	Name	Corps	Nature of casualty, or name of unit from or to which transferred	Date of being struck off or coming on the ration return	Remarks*
				Sick rejoined from Hospl:-		
				Other Ranks	8	
				Killed in Action :-		
				Officers	1	2. McLeod
				Sick admitted to Hospl:-		
				Other Ranks	9	
				Transfers to other Corps, ASC:-		
				Other Ranks	1	
				Draft from Base :-		
				Other Ranks	23	

* State whether absence is of a permanent or temporary nature, adding, in the case of casuals from wounds or disease, any available information for communication to the relatives.

Perforated Sheet giving detail of personnel and horses wanting to complete, shown on Army Form B. 213.

Number of Report _____

Remarks:—

Signature of Commander.

Unit.

Formation to which attached.

Date of Despatch.

[P.T.O.

Perforated Sheet giving detail of personnel and horses wanting to complete, shown on Army Form B. 213.

Number of Report _____

Detail of Wanting to Complete	Drivers						Gunners	Smith Gunners	Range Takers	Farriers		Shoeing, or Shoeing and Carriage Smiths	Cold Shoers	Wheelers			Saddlers or Harness Makers	Blacksmiths	Bricklayers and Masons	Carpenters and Joiners	Fitters & Turners (R. H.)		Fitters				Electricians		Signalmen	Engine Drivers		Air Line Men	Permanent Line Men	Operators, Telegraph	Cablemen	Brigade Section Pioneers	General-duty Pioneers	Signallers	Instrument Repairers	Motor Cyclists	Motor Cyclist Artificers	Telephonists	Clerks	Machine Gunners	Armament Artificers			Armourers	Storemen	Privates	W.O.'s and N.C.O.'s by ranks not included in trade columns	TOTAL wanting to agree with to complete		Horses			
	R. A.	R. E.	A. S. C.	Cart	Lorry	Steam				Sergeants	Corporals			R. A.	H. T.	M. T.					Wood	Iron	R. A.	Wireless	Plumbers	Ordinary	W. T.		Loco.	Field														Fitters	Range Finders						Officers	Other Ranks	Riding	Draught	Heavy Draught	Pack
CAVALRY																																																							
R. A.																																																		4					
R. E.																																																						
INFANTRY																																																						
R. A. M. C.																																																						
A. O. C.																																																						
A. V. C.																																																						

Remarks :—

_____ Signature of Commander.

_____ Unit.

_____ Formation to which attached.

_____ Date of Despatch. [P.T.O.

(82434.) Wt. 4394/2217. 500,000. 6/15. B.M.&S. Forms/B. 213/6.

Army Form B. 213.

FIELD RETURN.

No. of Report _____
(To be furnished by all arms, services, and departments (except A.S.C. units) to the A. G.'s Office at the Base in accordance with Field Service Regulations, Part II.)
RETURN showing numbers RATIONED by, and Transport on charge of, _____ at _____ Date _____

DETAIL	Personnel			Animals.							Guns, carriages, and limbers and transport vehicles			Horsed		Mechanical					REMARKS
	Officers	Other ranks	Natives	Horses			Mules		Camels	Oxen	Guns, carriages and limbers, showing description	Ammunition wagons and limbers	Machine guns	Aircraft, showing description	4 Wheeled	2 Wheeled	Motor Cars	Tractors	Lorries, showing description	Trucks, showing description	Trailers	Motor Bicycles	Bicycles
				Riding	Draught	Heavy Draught	Pack	Large	Small															
Effective Strength of Unit		25999			53	8	2					6	5	4		6	2							9
Details, by Arms attached to unit as in War Establishment:—																								
Total		25999			53	8	2					6	5	4		6	2							9
War Establishment		29995			55	8	2					6	5	4		6	2							9
Wanting to complete (Detail of Personnel and Horses below)	4	—																						
Surplus		4														1								
*Attached (not to include the details shown above)	×1	⊗3																						
Civilians:— Employed with the Unit Accompanying the Unit																								
TOTAL RATIONED ...		26607			53	8	2																	

* In the case of field ambulances, hospitals or depots, the number of patients are to be included here, the names being shown in A. F. A. 36.

_____ Signature of Commander.
_____ Date of Despatch.

For information of the A.G.'s Office at the Base.

Officers and men who have become casuals, been transferred or joined since last report.

Place On Service   Date 25.9.15

Regtl. Number	Rank	Name	Corps	Nature of casualty, or name of unit from or to which transferred	Date of being struck off or coming on the ration return	Remarks*
				Sick rejoined from Hospl		
				Other ranks	6	
				Sick admitted to Hospl		
				Other ranks	7	
				Interpreter Mr Le brun posted to A.Q. 8th Infy Bde	1	

* State whether absence is of a permanent or temporary nature, adding, in the case of casuals from wounds or disease, any available information for communication to the relatives.

81st Inf.Bde.
27th Div.

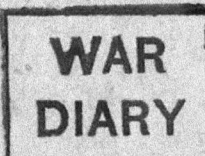

1st BATTN. THE ROYAL SCOTS.

OCTOBER

1 9 1 5

Attached:

Field Returns.

WAR DIARY
or
INTELLIGENCE SUMMARY

(Erase heading not required.)

Army Form 2118.

Hour, Date, Place	Summary of Events and Information	Remarks and references to Appendices
1.IX.15 MORCOURT	Company officers visited new trenches in the vicinity of CAPPY. Divisional Baths having been prepared, the men were able to have a much needed bath, but clean clothing was not available. The Companies made a number of brushwood hurdles.	Casualties: - 3.X.15 Capt. CLARK, 4Lt. BERRY and BUCHAN-HEPBURN to Hospital.
2.X.15	Bathing of Battalion completed. C.O. and 2nd in Command visited new trenches.	
4.X.15	Battalion marched to CAPPY, leaving MORCOURT at 6.30 am. Breakfasts at CAPPY. Companies proceeded independently to new trenches, relieving ROYAL IRISH REGT. These trenches had recently been taken over from the French and required much hard work to get them into satisfactory order. The so-called fire trenches were much trodden about by shell fire, mines etc. and consisted practically of a series of listening posts. The support line is the line of resistance. Communication	

Army Form 2118.

WAR DIARY
or
INTELLIGENCE SUMMARY
(Erase heading not required.)

Instructions regarding War Diaries and Intelligence Summaries are contained in F.S. Regs., Part II. and the Staff Manual respectively. Title pages will be prepared in manuscript.

Hour, Date, Place	Summary of Events and Information	Remarks and references to Appendices
	Trenches numerous and excellent in construction.	Casualties during period:- Wounded - 6 (1 accidentally)
6. X.15	One Company 8th R.S. Fusiliers attached for practical instruction in trench duties.	5th Oct. from England 2Lt. BULTEEL M.C.
8. X.15	Relieved by 2nd CAMERONS, and proceeded to billets in PROYART, remaining until the 12th inst. Battalion found two working parties of 200 men each, under R.E. Some of the Companies were billeted whilst at PROYART.	7th Lt. COCHRANE J.H. " CLIFFORD T.K. 7th Oct. from 14th B[tn]. R.S. 2 Lt. INNES J.R. " NOBLE A.
12. X.15	Relieved 2nd CAMERONS in the same trenches. Relief is easy, as it takes place during daylight.	Casualties during period Killed - 2 men Wounded - 8 men
16. X.15	Relieved by 8th SOUTH WALES BORDERERS, and marched independently to huts at FROISSY BRIDGE (cold and cheerless). During the last turn, the trenches were greatly improved and new communication trenches were opened up. On the 15th exchanged 4 platoon officers with similar number from 8th S.W.B.	

Army Form C. 2118.

WAR DIARY
or
INTELLIGENCE SUMMARY

(Erase heading not required.)

Instructions regarding War Diaries and Intelligence Summaries are contained in F. S. Regs., Part II. and the Staff Manual respectively. Title pages will be prepared in manuscript.

Hour, Date, Place	Summary of Events and Information	Remarks and references to Appendices
20.X.15	Some Corporals exchanged for temporary duty with a like number from the 8th S.W.B. Battalion relieved 8th S.W.B. in trenches.	Casualties:— Killed 1 man Wounded 1 man (accidental)
24.X.15	Relieved by trenches, and marched to billets in MORCOURT	
26.X.15	Battalion marched at 7.10 am to ST NICHOLAS (near AMIENS) and was under Canvas for that night, a distance of about 15 miles. The men behaved well.	
27.X.15	Marched to SAISSEMOND, a further 15 miles. Many men had new boots, others rode new ones, returned from many reasons etc, and the second day's march tried upon them. The roads were soft and much cut up by the R.A. and Train who preceded the Battalion	
31.X.15	The Battalion were still at SAISSEVAL. Since arrival the men have been exercised in marching, and minor tactical work.	Casualties:— 31.X.15 2/Lt. R.P. FLINT arrived from 2/ Entrenching Bn. Posted to B Co.

FIELD RETURNS.

Army Form B: 213.

FIELD RETURN.

No. of Report _____

(To be furnished by all arms, services, and departments to the A.G.'s Office at the Base in accordance with Field Service Regulations, Part II.)

RETURN showing numbers RATIONED by, and Transport on charge of _____ The 53rd Into at On Service _____ Date 2nd October 15.

DETAIL.	Personnel			Animals.							Guns, carriages, and limbers and transport vehicles				Horsed		Motor Cars	Tractors	Mechanical		Trucks, showing description	Trailers	Motor Bicycles	Bicycles	REMARKS
	Officers	Other ranks	Natives	Horses Riding	Draught	Heavy Draught	Pack	Mules Large	Small	Camels	Oxen	Guns, carriages and limbers, showing description	Ammunition wagons and limbers	Machine guns	Aircraft, showing description	4 Wheeled	2 Wheeled			Lorries, showing description					
Effective Strength of Unit	26	959			54	8			2			6	5	4		6	2							9	Numbers indicated but not right. See Officers 2 O.Ros 135
Details, by Arms attached to unit as in War Establishment:—																										
Total	26	989			54	8			2			6	5	4		62								9	
War Establishment	29	995			54	8			2			6	5	4		61								9	
Wanting to complete	3	6			-	-			-			-	-	-		-	1							-	
Surplus	-	-			-	-			-			-	-	-		1	-							1	
*Attached (not to include the details shown above)	*1 3																								x 1 Cook Name x 1 A.M.Sgt x 1 Sgt Shoemaker x 1 Horse Capt
Civilians:— Employed with the Unit Accompanying the Unit																									
TOTAL RATIONED	24	992			54	8			2																

Forms B. 213 / 5

* In the case of field ambulances, hospitals or depôts, the number of patients are to be included here, the names being shown in A.F.A. 36.

(Sgd) D.A. Callender Lt Col ___ Signature of Commander.

Comdg The 53rd Bath ___ Date of Despatch.

(K11889) W. & Co., Ltd. W1. w6506—894. 500,040. 10,14

For information of the A.G.'s Office at the Base.

Officers and men who have become casuals, been transferred or joined since last report.

Place **On Service**   Date **2nd Oct '15**

Regtl. Number	Rank	Name	Corps	Nature of casualty, or name of unit from or to which transferred	Date of being struck off or coming on the ration return	Remarks*
	Sick rejoined from Hosp¹					
	Other Ranks			7		
	Officers joined			1		To duty from [?]
	Sick admitted to Hosp¹					
	Other Ranks			14		
	Wounded (Accidentally Injured)					
	Other Ranks			1		To France
	To Base for Discharge					
	Other Ranks			2		[?]

*State whether absence is of a permanent or temporary nature, adding, in the case of casuals from wounds or disease, any available information for communication to the relatives.

Army Form B. 213.

FIELD RETURN.

No. of Report _____

(To be furnished by all arms, services, and departments to the A. G.'s Office at the Base in accordance with Field Service Regulations, Part II.)

Date _____ 9th Oct 18 _____

RETURN showing numbers RATIONED by, and Transport on charge of, _the total Scots_ at _by Service_

DETAIL	Personnel			Animals								Guns, carriages, and limbers and transport vehicles				Horsed		Mechanical					REMARKS
	Officers	Other ranks	Natives	Horses Riding	Horses Draught	Horses Heavy Draught	Pack	Mules Large	Mules Small	Camels	Oxen	Guns, carriages and limbers, showing description	Ammunition wagons and limbers	Machine guns	Aircraft, showing description	4 Wheeled	2 Wheeled	Motor Cars	Tractors	Lorries, showing description	Trucks, showing description	Trailers	Motor Bicycles	Bicycles	
Effective Strength of Unit Details, by Arms attached to unit as in War Establishment:—	30,987				52 8				2			6	5	4		6 2								9	Numbers included but not with Officer 1 126
Total	30,984				52 8				2			6	5	4		6 2								9	
War Establishment	29,995				54 8				2			6	5	4		6 1								9	
Wanting to complete	— 8				2				.			.	.	.		. 1								.	
Surplus	1																								
*Attached (not to include the details shown above)	1 3																								*1 Capt. R.A.M.C. 1 Lt O.M.Dept 1 Sgt Shoemaker 1 D. gun Coys
Civilians:— Employed with the Unit Accompanying the Unit																									
TOTAL RATIONED	31,990				52 8				2																

* In the case of field ambulances, hospitals or depôts, the number of patients are to be included here, the names being shown in A.F.A. 36.

Sgd. D. A. Callender Lt Col. Signature of Commander.
Comdg. The Total Scots

Date of Despatch.

Form B. 213/5

For information of the A.G.'s Office at the Base.

Officers and men who have become casuals, been transferred or joined since last report.

Place _On Service_   Date _9th Octr, 15_

Regtl. Number	Rank	Name	Corps	Nature of casualty, or name of unit from or to which transferred	Date of being struck off or coming on the ration return	Remarks*
		Drafts from U Kingdom				
		Officers			5	
		Convalescent Drafts from Base				
		Other Ranks			12	
		Sick Rejoined from Hosp.				
		Other Ranks			11	
		Officers Employed on Staff			1	2/Lt Lumsden as Bde Bomb Instr.
		Wounded, admitted to Hospital				
		Other Ranks			6	
		Sick admitted to Hospital				
		Other Ranks			19	

*State whether absence is of a permanent or temporary nature, adding, in the case of casuals from wounds or disease, any available information for communication to the relatives.

Army Form B. 213.

FIELD RETURN.

No. of Report _____

(To be furnished by all arms, services, and departments to the A.G.'s Office at the Base in accordance with Field Service Regulations, Part II.)

Date. 14th Oct. '15

RETURN showing numbers RATIONED by, and Transport on charge of, 1/5th The Loyal North Lancs, at _____

Detail.	Personnel			Animals								Guns, carriages, and limbers and transport vehicles					Mechanical					Remarks
	Officers	Other ranks	Natives	Horses Riding	Horses Draught	Horses Heavy Draught	Pack	Mules Large	Mules Small	Camels	Oxen	Guns, carriages, and limbers, showing description	Ammunition wagons and limbers	Machine guns	Aircraft, showing description	4 Wheeled Horsed	2 Wheeled Horsed	Motor Cars	Tractors	Lorries, showing description	Trucks, showing description	Trailers	Motor Bicycles	Bicycles	
Effective Strength of Unit	30	987		54	8	8		2	2			6	15	4		6	2							9	Numbers extended but not with Bn. Officers 9 O'ranks 122
Details by Arms attached to unit as in War Establishment:—																									
Total	30	987		54	8	8		2	2			6	15	4		6	2							9	
War Establishment	29	995		54	8	8		2	2			6	15	4		6	1							9	
Wanting to complete		12																							
Surplus	1																1								1 Officer attached R.E. +1 Capt. R.A.M.C. +1 R.Q.M. Sgt. +1 Sgt. Shoemaker +1 O. Corps Corpl
*Attached (not to include the details shown above)	× 1	× 3																							
Civilians:— Employed with the Unit Accompanying the Unit																									
Total Rationed	31	986		54	8	8		2	2																

* In the case of field ambulances, hospitals or depôts, the number of patients are to be included here, the names being shown in A.F.A. 36.

(Sgd.) L.A. Gallaher Lt. Col.
Comdg. 1/5th The Loyal N. Lancs.
Signature of Commander.

Date of Despatch.

For information of the A.G.'s Office at the Base.

Officers and men who have become casuals, been transferred or joined since last report.

Place On Service Date 16th Octr '15

Regtl. Number	Rank	Name	Corps	Nature of casualty, or name of unit from or to which transferred	Date of being struck off or coming on the ration return	Remarks*
		Reinforcement Drafts				
		Other Ranks			2	
		Sick rejoined from Hospl				
		Other Ranks			10	
		Killed in Action				
		Other Ranks			2	
		Wounded in Action				
		Other Ranks			8	
		Sick admitted to Hospl				
		Other Ranks			5	
		Class "A" Transfers to Base				
		Other Ranks			1	

*State whether absence is of a permanent or temporary nature, adding, in the case of casuals from wounds or disease, any available information for communication to the relatives.

Army Form B. 213.

FIELD RETURN.

No. of Report _____

(To be furnished by all arms, services, and departments to the A. G.'s Office at the Base in accordance with Field Service Regulations, Part II.)

Date. 27th October 15

RETURN showing numbers RATIONED by, and Transport on charge of, 1/4th Johnston at On Service

DETAIL	Personnel			Animals,							Guns, carriages, and limbers and transport vehicles										REMARKS
	Officers	Other ranks	Natives	Horses			Mules		Camels	Oxen	Guns, carriages and limbers, showing description	Ammunition wagons and limbers	Machine guns	Aircraft, showing description	Horsed		Motor Cars	Tractors	Mechanical			
				Riding	Draught	Heavy Draught	Pack	Large	Small							4 Wheeled	2 Wheeled			Lorries, showing description	Trucks, showing description	Trailers	Motor Bicycles	Bicycles	
Effective Strength of Unit Details, by Arms attached to unit as in War Establishment :—	29	949			55	8			2			6	5	4		6	2								9	9 Number is included but not with the Officers 1 O. Ranks 110
Total	29	949			55	8			2			6	5	4		6	2								9	
War Establishment	29	995			55	8			2			6	5	4		6	1								9	
Wanting to complete		16															1									
Surplus																										
*Attached (not to include the details shown above)	*1	3							2																	1 Officers Mess Cook 1 Batt. R.A.M.C 1 R.E.M. Sgt 1 Sub Shoemaker 1 O. Ranks Cpl
Civilians :— Employed with the Unit Accompanying the Unit																										
TOTAL RATIONED ...	30	932			55	8			2																	

* In the case of field ambulances, hospitals or depôts, the number of patients are to be included here, the names being shown in A.F.A. 36.

Maj S.A. Ballantyne ___ Signature of Commander.
Commdg. 1/4th Royal Scots Date of Despatch.

For information of the A.G.'s Office at the Base.

Officers and men who have become casuals, been transferred or joined since last report.

Place: On Service   Date: 23rd Octr. 18

Regtl. Number	Rank	Name	Corps	Nature of casualty, or name of unit from or to which transferred	Date of being struck off or coming on the ration return	Remarks*
Convalescent Draft from Base						
Other Ranks				5		
Sick rejoined from Hospital						
Other Ranks				13		
Posted to Staff, Other Corps						
Officers				1		Major Nargate to g—— Hrs. South Lancs Regt
Killed in Action						
Other Ranks				1		
Wounded in Action						
Other Ranks				1		
Sick admitted to Hospital						
Other Ranks				19		
Transferred to Base (Permanent)						Sgt. Christie to Office D.A.G. Base
Other Ranks				1		

*State whether absence is of a permanent or temporary nature, adding, in the case of casuals from wounds or disease, any available information for communication to the relatives.

Army Form B. 213.

FIELD RETURN.

No. of Report _____

(To be furnished by all arms, services, and departments to the A.G.'s Office at the Base in accordance with Field Service Regulations, Part II.)

RETURN showing numbers RATIONED by, and Transport on charge of _The Royal Scots_ at _On Service_ Date _30th October 1915_

Detail	Personnel			Animals								Guns, carriages, and limbers and transport vehicles							Mechanical				Motor Bicycles	Bicycles	Remarks
	Officers	Other ranks	Natives	Horses: Riding	Horses: Draught	Horses: Heavy Draught	Pack	Mules: Large	Mules: Small	Camels	Oxen	Guns, carriages and limbers, showing description	Ammunition wagons and limbers	Machine guns	Aircraft, showing description	Horsed 4-Wheeled	Horsed 2-Wheeled	Motor Cars	Tractors	Lorries, showing description	Trucks, showing description	Trailers			
Effective Strength of Unit Details, by Arms attached to unit as in War Establishment:—	29	946		5	51	7			2			6	5	4		6	2							9	9 Numbers included but not with the Battn. Officers 0 O. Ranks 51
Total	29	946		5	51	7			2			6	5	4		6	2							9	
War Establishment	29	995		5	51	8			2			6	5	4		6	1							9	
Wanting to complete		49		3		1																			
Surplus	1																1						1		
*Attached (not to include the details shown above)	*1	*5		1														1							*1 Sergt A.M.C. *1 R.M Sgt. *1 Sgt shoemaker *1 Officers Cook
Civilians:— Employed with the Unit Accompanying the Unit																									
Total Rationed ...	30	949		5	51	7			2																

* In the case of field ambulances, hospitals or depots, the number of patients are to be included here, the names being shown in A.F.A. 36.

Forms B. 213 / 5

(K 11869) W. & Co. Ltd. W₁ w6005-891 500,040 10.14

Signature of Commander _S.A. Callender Lt. Col._
Comdg. The Royal Scots
Date of Despatch _____

For information of the A.G.'s Office at the Base.

Officers and men who have become casuals, been transferred or joined since last report.

Place On Service Date 20th Octr '15

Regtl. Number	Rank	Name	Corps	Nature of casualty, or name of unit from or to which transferred	Date of being struck off or coming on the ration return	Remarks*
		Sick rejoined from Hospital				
		Other Ranks			12	
		Sick admitted to Hospital				
		Other Ranks			15	

*State whether absence is of a permanent or temporary nature, adding, in the case of casuals from wounds or disease, any available information for communication to the relatives.

www.ingramcontent.com/pod-product-compliance
Lightning Source LLC
Chambersburg PA
CBHW081555160426
43191CB00011B/1936